SUSTAINABLE WORLD

CITIES

Rob Bowden

KIDHAVEN
PRESS™

THOMSON
★
GALE

San Diego • Detroit • New York • San Francisco • Cleveland
New Haven, Conn. • Waterville, Maine • London • Munich

For more information, contact
KidHaven Press
27500 Drake Rd.
Farmington Hills, MI 48331-3535
Or you can visit our Internet site at http://www.gale.com

Commissioning Editor: Victoria Brooker
Book Designer: Jane Hawkins
Consultant: Dr. Rodney Tolley
Hodder Children's Books
A division of Hodder Headline Limited
338 Euston Road, London NW1 3BH

Book Editor: Margot Richardson
Picture Research: Shelley Noronha, Glass Onion Pictures

Cover: Housing in La Boca, Argentina.
Title page: Shanghai in China is one of the largest and fastest growing cities in the world.
Contents page: As San Salvador in El Salvador spreads outwards, housing extends on to new land.

Picture credits: Cover: Getty Images (Jochem D Wijnands); Andes Press Agency (Carlos Reyes-Manzo) 37; Brighton & Hove Council 41; Camera Press (Dolf Preisig) 8, 26; Chapel Studios (Zul Mukhida) 32; Corbis 35; Ecoscene (Matthew Bolton) 3, (Wayne Lawler) 5, (Wayne Lawler) 16, (Peter Currell) 18, (Tony Page) 19, (Tony Page) 27, (Guy Stubbs) 28, (Bruce Harber) 31, (Ray Roberts) 43; Panos Pictures (Mark Henley) 4, (Fred Hoogervorst) 6, (Giacomo Pirozzi) 7, (Chris Stowers) 10, (Trygve Bolstad) 11, (Fred Hoogervorst) 14, (Chris Stowers) 16, (Fred Hoogervorst) 17, (Paul Quayle) 20, (Penny Tweedie) 21, (Sean Sprague) 23, (Paul Smith) 24, (Paul Smith) 25, (Mark Hakansson) 29, (Daniel O'Leary) 33, 34, (Jeremy Horner) 38, (Crispin Hughes) 39, (Giacomo Pirozzi) 40, (Chris Stowers) 42; Rex Features 19; South American Pictures (Jason Howe) 36; Still Pictures (Harmut Schwarzbach) 9, (Paul Harrison) 12, (David Drain) 15, (John Maier) 25, (Ray Pforiner) 30; Växjö Energy Ltd/ Municipality of Växjö 22; Wayland 1, (Ville de Nice) 13, (White-Thomson Publishing) 44, (Steve Benbow) 45.

LIBRARY OF CONGRESS CATALOGING-IN-PUBLICATION DATA

Bowden, Rob
  Cities / by Rob Bowden.
    p. cm. — (Sustainable world)

Includes bibliographical references and index.
ISBN 0-7377-1901-X (hard : alk. paper)
Summary: Discusses the need for sustainable cities, the problems, ideas, solutions, and future of livable and healthy cities.
  1. Sustainable development. 2. Cities. 3. Growth planning. 4. Living conditions.
  I. Title. II. Sustainable World (Kidhaven Press)
HT155.B56 2004
  301.3—dc21

Contents

Why sustainable cities?

SOME TIME DURING 2007 the world will, for the first time, have as many urban residents as it does rural residents, an estimated 3.3 billion people! This massive concentration of people in urban centers is closely related to the growth in the global economy which is increasingly focused on the world's major cities. It is here that businesses and industries can operate more efficiently thanks to better communications, plenty of workers and suppliers, and an enormous market for their finished goods and services.

Tokyo, with 27 million people, is the world's largest city, and one of the most overcrowded.

FOR GOOD OR FOR BAD?

The development of the world's urban settlements, a process known as urbanization, has, however, been of mixed benefit. On one hand, cities makes infrastructure such as piped water, sewage systems, and transport networks cheaper than when people are spread out in rural areas. But cities create problems (such as pollution, overcrowding, congestion, and large amounts of waste) if they are not carefully planned, or happen too rapidly. Urbanization also has an impact on natural environments. For example, resources such as wood, food, and water are often extracted for use in cities while urban waste and pollution often flow back out. In addition, the very process of urbanization can destroy or change environments forever, such as the draining of wetlands for housing or industrial development.

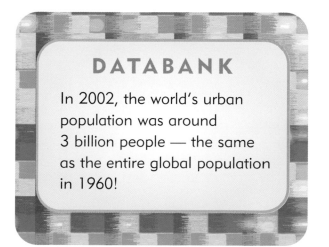

New houses built on greenbelt land around Edinburgh in Scotland show how urbanization is replacing natural environments.

OPINION

Within the next several years, more than half of us will be living in cities — making the world more urban than rural for the first time in history. We will have become an urban species, far removed from our hunter-gatherer origins.

Worldwatch Institute, 2000

MAKING URBANIZATION SUSTAINABLE

As urbanization continues, the proportion of the world's population living in cities is expected to exceed 60 percent by 2030. In the face of such growth there is an urgent need to consider how urbanization can be better managed to improve its sustainability. The challenge is to meet the everyday needs and hopes of urban people without harming the environment or living conditions of other people, both now and in the future. It is this idea of meeting today's needs while conserving resources for future generations that is the principle behind sustainable development. Already, this challenge is being taken up by some cities, but in others significant barriers and problems remain. This book will explore what sustainable urbanization might involve and how it might be achieved.

DATABANK

In 2002, the world's urban population was around 3 billion people — the same as the entire global population in 1960!

The challenge of sustainable cities

THE RAPID PACE OF urbanization presents numerous challenges to governments and the people living in cities. Not least among these challenges is the sheer size of some urban settlements, the largest of which (known as mega-cities) contain well over 10 million people. And in addition to environmental issues, there are considerable social, cultural, and political challenges that arise from having so many people living together. Some of the major challenges are further explored in this chapter.

OPINION

"Today's towns are tomorrow's cities; Today's cities are the future of mankind."

Urbanicity website

A slum area on the edge of Nairobi in Kenya. Kenya's towns and cities struggle to keep pace with the demand for housing and facilities.

KEEPING UP!

The proportion of people living in cities expanded dramatically during the twentieth century. In 1900, for example, less than 15 percent of the world's population lived in cities. By 1950 this had increased to almost 30 percent and had reached 47 percent by the turn of the millennium. By turning these percentages into real people — real mouths to feed, real homes to build, real demand for schools and hospitals — the challenge becomes more obvious. In 1950, for example, the world's urban population was around 0.75 billion, but by 2000 this had almost quadrupled to 2.9 billion. Most of this growth occurred in less-developed regions of the world such as Africa, Asia, and Latin America. In Asia, for example, the urban population increased by an incredible 1.13 billion people between 1950 and 2000, while in Africa it grew by 0.26 billion people over the same period.

Providing for such rapidly growing urban populations is a serious challenge for less developed countries, many of which are extremely poor. It is, however, in those very regions that urbanization is now most rapid and where most future growth in urban populations will occur.

A refugee camp of makeshift homes in Mauritania. Such settlements can add to the uncontrolled spread of urban areas.

Urban population by major world region 1950–2030 (in millions)

Region	1950	2000	2030 (predicted)
Africa	32.4	295.2	787.2
Asia	243.8	1,375.5	2,678.7
Europe	287.2	534.1	539.8
Latin America and the Caribbean	69.7	391.3	607.7
North America	109.7	243.0	335.0
Oceania	7.8	22.6	32.3
World	750.9	2,861.8	4,980.6

Source: UN Population Division
World Urbanization Prospects: The 2001 Revision

Congested urban roads, such as this highway in Los Angeles, have a major impact on the environment and people's health.

URBAN IMPACT

The urban population of more-developed regions is currently less than half that of less-developed regions. This does not make them any less important, however. In fact, it is in the urban areas of more-developed countries that some of the biggest impacts on sustainability could be made. This is because the greater wealth enjoyed by people living there means their consumption of resources, and therefore production of waste, is higher than in urban areas of less-developed countries. An average resident in the United States, for example, may use up to forty times more natural resources in their lifetime than a person in India. However, the impact of cities in less-developed regions is increasing and will surpass that of cities in more-developed regions unless more sustainable approaches to urbanization are adopted.

At a global level, cities are estimated to account for around 78 percent of carbon dioxide emissions, 76 percent of industrial wood use and 60 percent of fresh water consumption. And yet cities cover only around 2 percent of the earth's land surface.

ENGINES OF GROWTH

One of the main reasons for the disproportionate impact of cities on the environment is that they are at the center of the global economy; they are the engines of economic growth. It is in cities that most of the world's resources are converted into goods and services that are then traded around the world, often with other cities on the opposite side of the world. But, like any engine, cities demand large amounts of energy to function properly and produce vast quantities of waste. They also need a large workforce to keep them running and so attract people to urban areas in search of employment. It is no coincidence that the regions with the strongest and fastest growing economies are often those with the largest and fastest growing urban populations. In China, for example, where the economy is growing at around 10 percent a year, six hundred new cities are being built to help house the estimated 300 million people who will move from rural to urban areas by 2010.

OPINION

The cities of the twenty-first century are where human destiny will be played out, and where the future of the biosphere will be determined. There will be no sustainable world without sustainable cities.

Herbert Girardet,
Creating Sustainable Cities (1999)

weblinks

For more information on cities around the world, go to www.cities.com

Shanghai, China's largest city, grows increasingly upwards as land becomes more scarce.

DOES SIZE MATTER?

In 1950 New York was the only mega-city — a city with over 10 million inhabitants — in the world. By 2001, it had been joined by sixteen other cities, but had slipped back to fourth in size with a population of 16.8 million people. Above it in the list were Tokyo with 26.5 million people and Mexico City and Sao Paulo, Brazil, which both had a population of around 18.3 million. Besides being known for their incredible populations (Tokyo, for example, has more people than all Scandinavian countries combined) mega-cities are often used to demonstrate some of the problems associated with urbanization. Calcutta, India, is famous for its vast city slums, Los Angeles, California, for its traffic congestion, and Jakarta, Indonesia, and Manila, the Philippines, for their waste problems. So is it the sheer size of mega-cities that leads to such problems or is their reputation a little unfair?

Many urbanization experts argue that it is not the size of a settlement that matters, but the activities of the businesses, industries, and people living there. Further, they would argue that while historically cities have been the home of polluting industries and of people with higher incomes and therefore higher levels of consumption, this pattern is now changing.

DATABANK

Only around 4 percent of the world's population lives in urban centers with over 10 million people — the so-called mega-cities.

New York was the world's first mega-city and is still one of the largest cities in the world. But are such enormous cities sustainable?

Residents of suburbs, such as this near Oslo in Norway, often have a greater environmental impact than people living in urban centers.

weblinks

For more information about urbanization issues, go to www.urbancity.org

For example, many people with higher incomes now choose to live in rural areas or small towns beyond the city limits. By doing this, they normally increase their consumption of resources in comparison to people on similar incomes who remain living in the city. They may have two or three cars per household to meet their increased travel needs, such as traveling to school or work (which is often back in the urban centers). Their city equivalents may have no cars of their own and instead use public transport or even walk to get around.

In reality, then, the size of an urban area is not as significant as the way its people go about their daily lives. As we will discover, though, there is much that urban planners can do to help people make more sustainable choices.

Mega-cities in 2001

City, Country	Population (2001) in millions
Tokyo, Japan	26.5
Sao Paulo, Brazil	18.3
Mexico City, Mexico	18.3
New York, United States	16.8
Mumbai, India	16.5
Los Angeles, United States	13.3
Kolkata, India	13.3
Dhaka, Bangladesh	13.2
Delhi, India	13.0
Shanghai, China	12.8
Buenos Aires, Argentina	12.1
Jakarta, Indonesia	11.4
Osaka, Japan	11.0
Beijing, China	10.8
Rio de Janeiro, Brazil	10.8
Karachi, Pakistan	10.4
Manila, Philippines	10.1

Source: UN Population Division
World Urbanization Prospects: The 2001 Revision

These children in Jakarta, Indonesia, live and play among open canals contaminated with raw sewage and waste.

CITIES FOR PEOPLE

It is sometimes easy to forget that people are at the center of the urbanization process. For urbanization to become more sustainable, therefore, people must come first. Their need for homes, jobs, education, and healthcare must be met if they are to contribute to the prosperity and well-being of others and of the urban area as a whole. Failure to meet basic human needs can result in chaotic places where the health and safety of people is put at serious risk. For example, in many cities where the needs of the poor are ignored, crime has become a serious problem as they resort to illegal activities in order to

DATABANK

A third of the urban population in less-developed countries live in such poor quality environments that their lives and health are under constant threat.

survive. Cities such as Nairobi in Kenya, Johannesburg in South Africa, and Sao Paulo in Brazil are well known for their crime problems. In fact, the problem is so bad in Sao Paulo that murder is the biggest cause of death among men under thirty years of age. Improving the opportunities for people living in cities is a key challenge for the future.

Health is also important and is frequently linked to the state of the urban environment. Poor quality water supplies, inadequate waste control, and polluted air are all factors that can contribute to the ill-health of some urban populations, especially in less-developed countries. Children are especially at risk because their immune systems are less able to resist diseases and their developing bodies are more vulnerable to chemical pollutants emitted by industries or traffic. Improving the quality of urban environments and educating residents about how to prevent the spread of diseases will be essential to creating a more sustainable urban future.

CITIES FOR LIFE

Urbanization, though slowing, is here to stay. If carefully managed it can become a force for great good and the twenty-first century will be celebrated as the urban century. Not only can cities improve the use and efficiency of resources, they can also enrich the lives of people living there. For example, cities are centers for music, dance, theatre, art, and literature and many have famous cultural districts such as London's West End or Broadway in New York. Some have become famous cultural centers as a whole such as Florence in Italy, Barcelona in Spain, or Luxor in Egypt.

> ### OPINION
>
> If the urban future for much of the world is a continuation of what exists today, it is one in which millions of infants or children will die each year and tens of millions will have their physical and mental development impaired by avoidable or preventable diseases.
>
> *World Health Organization*
> *(WHO) 1996*

Festivals and carnivals such as this one in Nice, France, can be an enjoyable part of urban life.

Toward sustainable cities

A canal in Dhaka, Bangladesh, polluted with human waste. Many poor cities have no sewage system or toilets and so people use bags instead — known as a wrap and throw system!

THERE IS A LONG HISTORY of human effort to improve the health and well-being of urban populations. This is because, in the past, the high density of people living in a single location allowed diseases to spread with alarming speed and dramatic results. One of the best-known examples of this was the bubonic plague, in 1665, that killed an estimated one hundred thousand people in London. The plague was spread by fleas carried on London's teeming rat population which thrived on the city's poorly managed waste.

CLEANING THE CITIES

Other diseases common in urban areas were frequently connected to poor waste and water management. This was first realized in 1854, when a cholera epidemic in London was traced to a drinking well that had been contaminated by human sewage. Following this discovery, city authorities constructed sewers to handle waste and built water treatment plants to

New laws have helped clean urban air, but water pollution remains a problem in industrial cities such as at this steel works in Spain.

remove harmful bacteria and other disease causing agents from drinking water supplies. Disease and death rates fell dramatically as a result, proving that there was a positive link between the quality of urban environments and the health of their populations.

Throughout the twentieth century, further measures have been taken to improve urban environments and health. These include clean air acts to ban the burning of smoky fuels such as coal, and the introduction of unleaded gasoline to reduce rates of lead poisoning among urban children. However, while most cities in more-developed countries today enjoy the benefit of such actions, many people in less-developed countries still suffer from poor urban environments and high rates of disease.

WIDER IMPACT

Despite the progress made in cleaning up urban environments, there has been less progress in tackling the broader environmental impacts of urban areas, such as their consumption of resources (trees, water, food, etc.) from surrounding areas. In fact, it has taken a lot longer for such impacts to even be recognized, let alone dealt with. During the 1960s, however, as concerns about the environment gathered strength, people began to examine cities more closely. They discovered that cities, and urban areas in general, were disrupting or at worst destroying their surrounding environments. They also found that as urban areas grew, their influence extended further and further afield, affecting ever more people and previously untouched environments. Suddenly there was a new impetus to reduce the impact of the world's cities and their ever-growing populations.

URBAN ECOLOGY

One of the main changes that has taken place in recent years is the consideration of cities as living organisms that consume resources and produce wastes like all other organisms on earth. This approach is sometimes known as urban ecology and has become a major focus in the quest for sustainable urbanization.

The problem with most cities is that they function as what ecologists call linear systems. This means that resources flow through them with little thought as to where they have come from or where the wastes they generate might end up. Such linear systems are very different to natural ecosystems, which are circular systems with resources and wastes being continually recycled. In this way the wastes from one part of the system become the resources for another and the whole system is maintained over time. This is the principle of sustainability.

Right: This Australian rainforest continually recycles itself.
Below: Timber extracted from surrounding forests is traded in Jakarta, Indonesia.

Polluted water pours into the Indian Ocean outside Karachi, Pakistan.

Based on such an understanding, it is now recognized that cities should function more like the circular ecosystems found in nature if they are to become sustainable. The problem, however, is that cities can never be truly self-sufficient in the same way that natural ecosystems are. Most draw on resources (such as food) from far beyond their immediate environment and produce wastes that are deposited in and influence distant places. And the reach of cities is increasing as improvements in transport and communications allow their populations to utilize resources from ever more distant locations.

RETHINKING URBANIZATION

With urbanization having such wide-reaching effects it has become clear that major changes are needed. These must not only address local issues, but rethink the entire organization of urban living and its connections with regional and global environments. Such actions will require physical changes in the way that cities function but, perhaps more importantly, they must be accompanied by changes in the way their inhabitants live. For example, people will have to reduce their consumption of energy and resources and increase their rates of recycling in order to reduce the waste they generate.

---

weblinks

For more information about the environment and urbanization, go to www.iied.org

The city of Toronto in Canada has an impact on
the environment that extends way beyond the
city boundaries.

ECOLOGICAL FOOTPRINTS

An interesting approach to looking at the
impact of cities is the idea of ecological
footprints. An ecological footprint measures how much productive land is needed
to provide the residents of any particular
area (such as a city) with the resources they
consume and to absorb the wastes they
produce. (Although ecological footprints
measure the resources cities need, they do
not deal with issues such as the damage
done to ecosystems by chemicals and other
wastes.)

Several studies have used ecological
footprints to produce some fascinating
results. In Canada, for example, a study
revealed that the residents of Toronto,
Ontario, which covers an area of 240
square miles, required 48,800 square
miles to meet their resource and waste
needs. This means that the ecological
footprint of Toronto is 200 times greater
than its actual geographic area. London's
ecological footprint has been measured at
125 times its actual size, while in Van-
couver, British Columbia, it has been measured at 180 times its area.

A totally self-sufficient and sustainable
city would have a footprint of one, but in
reality no city could achieve this. Cities
can reduce their ecological footprints
dramatically, however, especially if they
are able to see how their footprint is made
up. In London, for example, it has been
estimated that 26 percent of resource use
(excluding water) and 73 percent of waste

Top: Many of London's buildings are lit up at night, needlessly using energy.
Above: People living in this low-income district of Santiago, Chile, have less impact on the environment than their wealthier neighbors.

generation is caused by energy consumption. Introducing energy conservation measures and converting to renewable forms of energy that produce substantially less waste could therefore dramatically reduce the overall footprint of the city.

BIG FEET, LITTLE FEET

The development of the ecological footprint approach has made a great contribution to the study of sustainable urbanization, but many experts warn that it must be used with caution. Like other statistics it is only an indicator of sustainability and, more importantly, it often ignores the variation in impact that different groups within the city might have. Some will have a much bigger footprint than others. In Santiago, the capital of Chile, a study was conducted to demonstrate this difference. It found that one of Santiago's wealthiest districts (Vitacura) had a footprint around forty times bigger than one of its poorest districts (Cerro Navia). This was despite the population of Cerro Navia being almost twice that of Vitacura.

DEVELOPMENT

Millions of urban residents in Africa and Asia have no access to piped water in their homes. Instead, as in this part of Mumbai, India, water must be collected from standpipes in the street.

The development part of sustainable development is often forgotten. Development is about improving people's living conditions and lives, such as providing access to water and sanitation, or ensuring that people can afford to send their children to school. These issues are as important as the sustainability side of sustainable development but are frequently ignored or overlooked. In Santiago, for example, the residents of Cerro Navia may have a small ecological footprint, but they should not be expected to remain living in poverty in order to maintain it. They require better homes, improved livelihoods, and the ability to enjoy a lifestyle nearer to that of their wealthier neighbors in Vitacura. It is therefore vital that one of the priorities for sustainable urbanization should be to raise the quality of life for hundreds of millions of urban residents living in poor accommodation with few facilities and a lack of economic opportunities.

A BALANCING ACT

Current patterns of urbanization suggest that as the wealth and quality of life of urban residents improves, their consumption of resources and generation of waste increases. Finding solutions that improve urban lives without increasing their environmental impact is a complicated and delicate balancing act. People will certainly have to adapt their lifestyles in many parts of the world, but this need not involve a reduction in quality of life or wealth. In fact, many measures would improve both the quality and costs of urban living dramatically. In many instances, technology is helping to provide more sustainable solutions to everyday needs. For example, Compact Fluorescent Lamps (CFL) use only a quarter of the energy of a normal light bulb and last up to ten times as long. Similarly, a low-flow cistern on a toilet can reduce water use by around 70 percent. Between 1994 and 1997, New York reduced water consumption by up to 90,000,000 gallons a day following the introduction of 1.33 million low-flow toilets. Simple examples like this show that it is possible to promote development while making sure that it is sustainable.

Persuading people to change their lifestyles is a more delicate matter. For example, getting people to actively recycle, even if they know about the benefits, is a significant challenge. Creating awareness and greater cooperation among national governments, local authorities, and communities will be crucial to the long term success of sustainable urbanization.

Recycling household waste in Alberta, Canada, is one way to adopt a more sustainable lifestyle.

Sustainable cities in practice

The city of Växjö, Sweden, is supplied with electricity and heat generated by burning waste from the forestry industry.

THERE ARE ENCOURAGING EXAMPLES around the world that give reason for great optimism about the future sustainability of cities. They show that at a variety of scales, from the individual home to the entire city, things can be done to improve the well-being of the people living there while maintaining, or even improving the natural environment. As this chapter will show, some measures are relatively simple, but others have involved a major shift in the way urban areas function. Both are just as important and both provide valuable lessons for the future.

CLOSING THE CIRCLE

There is much that can be done in existing urban areas to make them function more like natural ecosystems and dramatically improve their sustainability (see page 16). This is sometimes referred to as closing the circle. Changes in energy policies could have a dramatic impact, for example. In 1996, the city authorities of Växjö, Sweden, announced plans to eliminate the use of

Human waste, carried to fields in China, is a sustainable method of disposal.

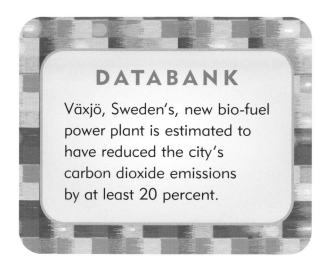

fossil fuels, and so reduce greenhouse gas emissions, by converting to renewable energy sources. At the center of their policy is the use of bio-fuels to generate electricity, such as wood waste from the forestry industry. The heat produced in this process is also used to heat buildings and homes in the city via a district heating system. As long as trees are replanted at the same rate (or greater) as they are felled, then this is a highly sustainable method of energy production.

Electricity and heat are generated in other cities by the burning of municipal waste. In Amsterdam, The Netherlands, for example, some trams now run on electricity generated from the city's own waste. Urban waste can also be used to replace resources, such as food, extracted from surrounding rural areas. In Kano, Nigeria, for example, urban waste is delivered to farmers in the surrounding rural districts. The farmers sort the waste, separating out organic content such as vegetable waste and donkey manure (donkeys are used to transport goods within the city) for use as a fertilizer on their fields. The nutrients in the waste replace those lost when food is taken from the fields to feed urban populations. A similar practice has existed in China for thousands of years, where each morning chamber pots (a form of toilet) are taken from settlements to be emptied on to nearby fields as a type of natural fertilizer.

OPINION

In a sustainable system there is no waste, but wherever there are humans, waste is produced. The second best option to no waste is to create an ecological cycle with a minimum of resources.

City of Stockholm website

Curitiba, Brazil, has a highly efficient bus system that is central to its planning for a sustainable city. It has since been modeled elsewhere.

PLANNING FOR SUSTAINABILITY

Several cities around the world have gained a reputation as the eco-cities of the future. In many instances their success has demanded a complete reorganization of the way cities are managed and run. One of the best known eco-cities is Curitiba in southern Brazil. When faced with a rapidly growing population in the 1960s, Curitiba began a careful process of planning a sustainable city. At the center of the plan was a highly efficient city transit system based on giving buses priority over cars and making sure that all parts of the city were easily connected to the bus network. The transit system now carries 2 million people a day, has reduced traffic by 30 percent and given Curitiba the cleanest air in urban Brazil.

Curitiba's planners have also created a people-friendly city. Downtown areas have been pedestrianized and green spaces developed to raise the quality of the urban environment itself. In fact, the network of parks and wooded areas has increased green space in the city by fifty-two times per person since 1970, even though the population has doubled in that time. Waste management is also important and today around 70 percent of the city's waste is recycled.

THE CITY OF ALL OF US

The key to Curitiba's success has been its inclusion of all urban dwellers. In fact, it is called "the city of all of us." For example, the bus system operates on a flat-rate social fare. This means that the poorer residents who live toward the edge of the city pay no more for a ticket than wealthier residents living nearer to the center. Waste management also focuses on inclusion. The poorer shanty areas of the city are harder for garbage trucks to reach, and so their residents are encouraged to bring their waste to neighboring collection points. In return they receive vouchers for food or bus tickets for the transit system. Children are also encouraged to participate by collecting recyclable garbage and exchanging it for school supplies, toys, or even chocolate. Not only does this help manage waste now, but also teaches children the value and importance of recycling.

Right: Residents from the poorer regions of Curitiba, Brazil, line up to exchange waste they have collected in exchange for food. Such programs benefit people and the environment. Below: Street children in Curitiba contribute to the future of their city by helping to maintain the city parks and gardens.

> ## OPINION
>
> Services like parks and high quality public transportation give dignity to the citizens and if people feel respected they will assume responsibility to help solve other problems.
>
> *Jamie Lerner,*
> *former mayor of Curitiba, Brazil*

SETTING THE STANDARD

A resident looks over the district of Hammarby Sjöstad in Stockholm, Sweden. It is designed to be a completely sustainable part of the city.

Creating sustainable cities on the scale of Curitiba is not always possible. In many countries, cities have been established for much longer and do not have the flexibility to plan in the way that Curitiba has been able to, and continues to do. However, there are several examples of how cities are taking advantage of redevelopment opportunities to create more sustainable solutions to urban living.

For example, in Sweden, Hammarby Sjöstad, a district of the capital, Stockholm, is being transformed into a modern, ecologically sustainable part of the city. When it is completed in 2010, the old docks and industrial areas will have been redeveloped into a city in which thirty thousand people can live and work. Trams, walkways, bicycle paths, and car pools will provide sustainable transportation links to other parts of Stockholm. Within Hammarby Sjöstad itself the aim is to minimize the use of resources from beyond the district. It also aims to use eco-cycle technologies that mimic natural ecosystems. For example, sewage and organic waste from the district will be broken down to produce bio-gas that can be used to fuel ovens, heat water, and even power vehicles.

In the United Kingdom, the BedZED (Beddington Zero Energy Development) project shows that it is possible to design urban settlements that do not add carbon dioxide to the atmosphere. This is achieved by using the latest environmental building designs and generating electricity onsite using bio-fuels and solar panels. In addition to being self-sustaining in energy, BedZED recycles rainwater and grey water (domestic waste water) using its Living Machine — a system of reed and gravel beds that filter and clean the water. This water is then used for flushing toilets. Transportation is also an important consideration of the project. There is a car pool of forty electric cars that are recharged by photovoltaic (PV) cells on the roofs of the buildings, and secure bicycle storage is provided to encourage cycling. Work space, connected to the homes, is also provided to try to reduce the need to travel at all. People who want both home and work space are given priority over others to live there.

In addition to its ecological achievements, the BedZED project will also include homes for those less able to afford them, with twenty-five of the eighty-two housing units set aside for assisted housing that is partly paid for by the government. BedZED may be small scale, but like Hammarby Sjöstad it is helping to set the standard for urban living in the twenty-first century.

The BedZED project near London in the United Kingdom shows how homes may change in the future.

weblinks

To find out more about the BedZED project go to www.BedZED.org.uk

OPINION

It's good to see such an enthusiastic response to the BedZED concept. It is clear that there are many people eager and willing to opt for a more sustainable lifestyle.

Richard McCarthy, Chief Executive, The Peabody Trust

URBAN SELF-SUFFICIENCY

A truly self-sufficient city is an ambitious target. However, there are ways in which cities can improve their self-sufficiency. One of the most widespread of these is the practice of urban agriculture: the growing or production of food in an urban or semi-urban (often called peri-urban) environ-

ment. This might seem a strange concept, but if you live in an urban area you can probably find evidence of this for yourself. Public gardens, for example, are a common sight in many cities, while other people set aside part of their own gardens to grow fruit and vegetables such as apples, strawberries, beans, or tomatoes.

In more-developed regions of the world, growing food in urban areas is often a leisure activity that people enjoy and use to supplement their diets. In less-developed countries, however, urban agriculture can be a vital source of food, especially for poorer residents. Food is frequently among the most expensive elements of urban living for poor households in less-developed countries, accounting for over half of their

DATABANK

In large Chinese cities 90 percent or more of vegetable needs are met by urban and semi-urban farming.

Urban farming, such as this in South Africa, helps make towns and cities self-sufficient.

Using fertilizer made from sewage, fish are farmed in the wetlands surrounding Calcutta, one of India's biggest cities.

income. Growing your own food, therefore, becomes a sensible choice. In Kenya, a study of six towns found that two-thirds of households were partly producing their own food. In Lusaka, the capital of Zambia, around half of low-income households are estimated to be using vacant plots of land for urban agriculture. Urban agriculture is not always about crops, either. In Uganda it is common to see livestock such as chickens, goats, and cattle within and around the edge of urban centres. In Calcutta, India, around 7,500 tons of fish are reared annually in urban ponds fertilized by sewage from the city population. The sewage is also used to fertilize farms that produce some 150 tons of vegetables every day.

Despite its benefits for sustainability, many urban authorities discourage or even ban urban agriculture believing it to be a rural activity. In some cities it is now being given active support, however. In Santiago de los Caballeros in the Dominican Republic, the city authorities have now included urban farming in their land-use planning. They are identifying available land to increase the 19 percent of the urban area already farmed and have established projects to demonstrate urban farming techniques such as composting.

weblinks

To find out more about urban agriculture go to www.cityfarmer.org

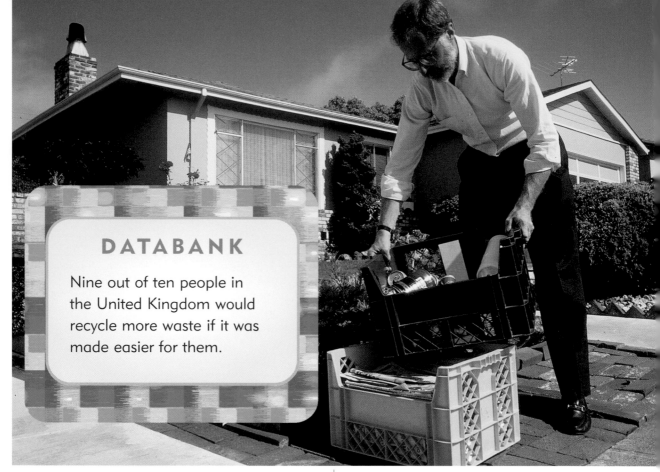

CREATING OPPORTUNITIES

Curbside recycling programs, such as here in California, can help to improve the sustainable management of urban waste.

Across the world, urban residents show a willingness to improve the condition of their environments and make their lifestyles more sustainable. Too often, however, they lack the opportunities to turn their willingness into positive actions. Even simple measures such as recycling household waste can be difficult in areas where local authorities do not assist. In the United Kingdom, for example, recycling glass, paper, clothes, and tin cans is now relatively easy with collection bins at supermarkets and in town centers. However, plastic and cardboard, which make up a large proportion of packaging materials, plus used oil and batteries, are harder to recycle with relatively few collection centers. Similarly, recycling organic waste, which could be composted, is not easy for urban residents who lack the space for a composting bin or cannot use the compost once it is made.

Recycling programs such as curbside collections can dramatically increase rates of urban recycling, but in the United Kingdom at least, less than half of households currently have such programs and many of those only take selected items.

Urban authorities could also create more sustainable transportation choices by investing in cycling and pedestrian facilities, and well-connected public transportation links. Several European nations are leading the way with such programs. Denmark, Germany, The Netherlands, Sweden, and Austria have all achieved impressive results in encouraging people to abandon their cars and switch to more sustainable alternatives. In the German city of Freiburg, for example, a quarter of all journeys are now made by bicycle, while in Copenhagen, Denmark, over 34 percent of home-to-work journeys are made by bicycle. Copenhagen's cycle program even includes the free use of around 2,000 city-bikes that are distributed at special cycle stands around the city. Users simply pay a small deposit when they collect their city-bike which is repaid when they park at the stand nearest to their destination. This relatively simple program ensures that even the least wealthy members of society can use sustainable transportation options. Such programs are role models for other towns and cities around the world that are looking to become more sustainable.

— weblinks —

To learn more about Copenhagen's City-Bike program go to
www.bycyklen.dk/engelsk/frameset.html

A public bicycle-share program in Denmark helps to reduce the need for motorized transportation in cities.

Creating sustainable cities

MANAGING AN URBAN AREA is a serious challenge, especially in today's modern mega-cities. Imagine, for example, running a city the size of Tokyo. In terms of population this would be like being the president or prime minister of the whole of Scandinavia! Leaders such as Jamie Lerner, the former mayor of Curitiba, Brazil, have shown, however, that with strong leadership impressive results can be achieved. Similar leadership has been responsible for many of the examples we have learned about in this book. So what is it that determines whether or not urbanization follows a sustainable path?

Residents of Nakuru, Kenya, have shown a willingness to improve their city, but lack the financial support to turn ideas into realities.

POWER TO CHOOSE

Giving urban authorities the power to make decisions is one of the most important factors in determining the success of any policy. This power should include not only the political power to make decisions, but also the financial power to control their own budgets. In many countries such power is held mainly at the national level and urban authorities find themselves competing with other causes for a share of the available funds. In Nakuru, Kenya, for example, a strong local network is committed to improving

Ahmedabad, India, has benefited by having greater control of its own budget. Managing cities locally is a key to their sustainable future.

OPINION

'If cities are properly managed, with adequate attention paid to social development and the environment, the problems present as a result of rapid urbanization, particularly in developing regions, can be avoided.'

UN Environment Program, Global Environment Outlook (GEO) 3

urban environments and welfare, but is hampered by a lack of funding from the central government.

In contrast to Nakuru, the city of Ahmedabad in India has control of its own budget and relies on the central government for only 10 percent of its funding. Greater control has allowed the city to develop projects that suit its particular needs. During the period of 1993–2002 alone the Ahmedabad Municipal Corporation (AMC) has succeeded in providing safe water supplies to the city, reducing traffic congestion, and improving living conditions in the city's slum settlements. More importantly, though, AMC succeeded in gaining the confidence and support of its citizens by creating a modern and efficient management team.

Gaining the support of urban residents in this way helps to strengthen local democracies — a vital contribution to the success of any new policies. With strong democracies people can feel confident that the contributions they are asked to make toward the running of the city (in the form of taxes, for example) are being properly spent and not wasted on administration or corrupt officials.

PEOPLE POWER

In places where urban authorities lack sufficient power or funds to make changes, local people have often taken things into their own hands. The power of local people to make positive changes to cities may not receive much attention, but their efforts often result in considerable benefits for people and the environment. One of the best examples of people power comes from Orangi, a township in Karachi, Pakistan, that is home to about 1.2 million people. Orangi began as an informal settlement in 1965, with its population boosted by the arrival of refugees from Bangladesh in 1972. The settlement was largely unplanned with poor quality housing, no sanitation system, and hardly any piped water.

In 1980, a retired rural development adviser realized that with no power to influence government authorities, the people of Orangi would have to help themselves if they wanted to improve their living conditions. He formed the Orangi Pilot Project (OPP) to gather the residents into local committees organized by lanes within the township. Each lane was encouraged to raise funds and to help build and maintain their own section of a sewer system connected to sanitary pour-flush latrines in their homes. To date, close to six thousand lanes have developed their own sewer system serving over ninety thousand households. The main reason why low-income households could take part was that the work cost around $30 per household, one-sixth of what it would have cost if undertaken by the state.

The Orangi Pilot Project is now being modeled in eight other cities in Pakistan (such as Faisalabad, shown here) and in forty-nine other settlements in Karachi.

OPINION

'The poor of cities are not just passive objects. Most often they are solving their own problems. So if you listen...the people themselves would solve most of the problems.'

Anna Tibaijuka,
Executive Director of UN-Habitat

Technological and financial innovations were the easy part; the difficult part was in convincing residents that they could and should invest in their own sanitation systems. Although initially developed outside of government, the OPP encourages the government to take responsibility, often with the inhabitants managing the construction of the latrines, lane sewers, and small secondary sewers and the government providing the larger sewers, and treatment plants. In total, the residents of Orangi have spent some $1.4 million on improving their own neighborhood.

The biggest impacts of the OPP have been on the health and well-being of the residents, though. Infant mortality rates, for instance, have fallen from 13 percent in 1982 to less than 3.7 percent today. This is lower than the national average of 9.5 percent. Other benefits include the

Improved education levels are one of several benefits felt by the people of Orangi, Pakistan, as a result of improvements to their town.

creation of new jobs, fewer neighborhood disputes (often caused by the filthy living conditions), and a 15–20 percent increase in the value of properties in Orangi.

PARTNERSHIPS FOR PROGRESS

One of the benefits of urbanization as far as sustainability is concerned, is that it brings diverse groups of people together in a single location. They represent different ideas, concerns, skills, and abilities which, if combined, can work for the benefit of all. Partnerships for sustainable urbanization are now emerging throughout the world and achieving considerable success in many locations.

In Bogotá, Colombia, for example, the city authorities are working in partnership with private bus operators in their ambitious aim to reduce private car use. Prior to the partnership, Bogotá's streets were congested with thousands of old, polluting buses that provided an unreliable service because they were competing with cars for road space. In 1998, the mayor

New buses have helped transform public transportation in Bogotá, Colombia, and contributed to a cleaner, healthier, and less congested city.

Residents of Port Alegre, Brazil, meet to discuss and make decisions about the future of their city and how its money should be spent.

PARTICIPATION

announced ambitious plans to launch a new, rapid bus service following the example of Curitiba (see pages 24–5) in Brazil. The city provided the infrastructure such as special bus lanes, passenger stations, bus maintenance facilities, and pedestrian access and also purchased a fleet of cleaner, more efficient buses. The private bus operators could then bid for the buses and routes that would make up the new system. The first buses went into service in December 2000 and within a year were carrying six hundred thousand passengers a day. By 2002 this had increased further to an estimated eight hundred thousand and the system had gained worldwide praise as an example of a partnership for progress. The city authorities have also developed an extensive network of bicycle paths.

Besides partnerships between authorities and private companies it is important that residents themselves participate in deciding their future sustainability. In Porto Alegre, Brazil, the city authorities have introduced a system of participatory budgeting that allows residents from all sectors of the city to have a say in how the city budget is spent, including how it is spent in their neighorhood. Elected officials meet with residents' groups from each region of the city to discuss what they consider to be the main priorities. Across the city this process involves some thirty thousand people each year and has been so successful that a further fifty cities in Brazil now use participatory budgeting methods. So partnerships and participation certainly appear to benefit urban areas, but focusing their energy toward sustainable urbanization is another challenge altogether.

LOCAL AGENDA 21

At the 1992 Earth Summit in Rio de Janeiro, Brazil, world leaders met to discuss how to make development more sustainable in the future. By the end of the summit, governments had agreed on a plan for achieving sustainable development known as Agenda 21 (21 referring to the twenty-first century). In addition, each country and localities (such as cities) within each country were to develop their own plans of action known as a Local Agenda 21 or LA21.

The need to develop LA21s provides urban authorities and their populations with a focus for achieving sustainable urbanization but, to date, experiences have been mixed. Many LA21s have proved to be weak plans that ignore the views and wishes of urban residents, and especially groups such as the poor and the young. There are, however, more successful examples of LA21s, many of which come from less-developed countries. For example, in Peru, LA21s have helped to transform the cities of Ilo and, to a lesser extent, Chimbote, reducing air pollution and water contamination and improving the quality of urban housing for the poor. In Manizales, Colombia, the LA21 process led to an innovative idea of environmental traffic lights. They are positioned in public areas and inform residents of the progress being made in improving the environment in each neighborhood. A red light warns that things are getting worse, orange shows that they are about the same, while green shows that conditions are improving.

SHARING FOR THE FUTURE

Successful LA21s have normally been where residents participate in the process, and information, ideas and results are openly shared. The sharing of information is also important at an international level so that urban authorities can learn from the successes and failures of others. Several networks now allow towns and cities to compare their experiences and find appropriate solutions to their problems.

There is also a human settlements program within the United Nations. Known as UN-Habitat, this program was set up in 1978 to help the world community work together for sustainable urbanization. UN-Habitat works with everyone involved in urban development, from national governments to local slum dwellers. In 2002, for example, it brought together over twelve hundred representatives (including two hundred slum dwellers) from eighty countries in the first ever World Urban Forum. The experiences and ideas from the forum will help UN-Habitat to improve its work toward the goal of sustainable urbanization.

OPINION

'City-to-city cooperation adds a new dimension to the learning process. Given their increasing power and influence, cities are beginning to recognize the importance of working together to face common challenges.'

Kofi Annan, UN Secretary General

weblinks

To learn more about the work of UN-Habitat go to www.unhabitat.org

MAKE YOUR TOWN A green TOWN

Raising awareness of urban issues and encouraging people to think about solutions is of great importance to sustainable urbanization.

Sustainable cities and you

THE SCALE OF URBANIZATION CAN make it seem like there is little that individuals like you and me can do. This could not be further from the truth, however, because urban centers are simply collections of individuals making their own decisions as they go about their daily lives. If proof were needed that individuals can make a difference then you need only look back at some of the examples we have learned about in this book. For example, the sanitation project in Orangi, Pakistan; the state-of-the-art bus system in Bogotá, Colombia; or the sustainable city of Curitiba, Brazil. Each of these owes its success to individuals who recognized the challenges of sustainable urbanization and encouraged those around them to do something about it.

Women in Cape Town, South Africa, work together on a construction project to improve their neighborhood.

Young people from Brighton and Hove in the United Kingdom sort bottles for recycling as part of a program to improve their urban environment.

LEAD BY EXAMPLE

As we have seen, there is much that urban residents around the world can do to contribute toward a more sustainable future. Many of the measures are very simple. For example, energy reductions and water conservation are measures that virtually every household is able to make. Other measures may be more challenging, but are still relatively simple to achieve. Recycling, for example, could dramatically reduce the amount of waste that is produced and simply involves sorting waste into different materials such as paper, glass, and plastics. Trials in the United Kingdom show that when shown how to separate waste properly, a typical urban household can recycle at least 90 percent of its waste.

Transportation is an area where most urban residents or visitors can contribute to sustainability. By walking, cycling, or using public transportation instead of private vehicles, people will not only reduce the amount of energy they consume (in the form of fuel), but help reduce air pollution and improve their own health too! Urban journeys are often relatively short, so making such changes to travel habits is not difficult in most cases.

There are many other ways in which individuals can contribute toward sustainable urbanization. You can probably think of your own ideas, having read this book, but to help you consider what other actions you could take, a few more suggestions are listed on the next page.

Walking is not just good for urban environment, it is also good for your health and gives you time to socialize with friends.

LOCAL ACTION
You can make a difference

- Save energy by turning off appliances and lights when not needed.

- Encourage your parents to look at making your own home more sustainable.

- Separate and recycle your waste and reduce the amount generated in the first place.

- Use sustainable transportation methods (including walking!) in urban areas.

- Find out about Local Agenda 21 in your area and find out how to join in.

- Suggest that your school set up a project to study sustainable urbanization.

- If you have space, think about growing some of your own food.

RURAL AREAS

Many of the suggestions on the left also apply to people living in rural settlements and their actions are just as important in making a difference. For example, they might plan their trips into neighboring urban areas more carefully to reduce the number of journeys needed. They could also make the journey by public transportation or, if they have to use their own vehicle, offer a lift to friends, family, or neighbors.

ACT NOW!

Many people believe they are powerless to make a difference about big issues such as urbanization and so do nothing. An example from Brazil shows that this is far from true. Since 1998, children from nine to fifteen were given responsibility for around $125,000 of the city budget for Barra Mansa, Brazil. The children of Barra Mansa elect eighteen boys and eighteen girls as their city council members. These then work with other parts of the local government and different urban neighborhoods to decide how the budget should be spent to meet children's urban needs. Such circumstances can give children an influential role in choosing policies that guide cities toward a more sustainable future.

You may not be able to participate in such a council, but you can still act now. For example, you could work with friends to create a Local Agenda 21 for improving the sustainability of your school. You could even make your own environmental traffic lights like those in Manizales (see page 38) to monitor the progress being made toward your agreed targets.

weblinks

To learn more about the work of Local Agenda 21, go to www.scream.cok.ik/la21

For those who have the space, producing food can make a positive contribution to urban sustainability. It can also be very rewarding.

OPINION

The urban century offers us considerable problems, but it also offers us hope, and the prospect of trying to find the solutions together.

Felix Dodds, UN Environment and Development Program, United Kingdom

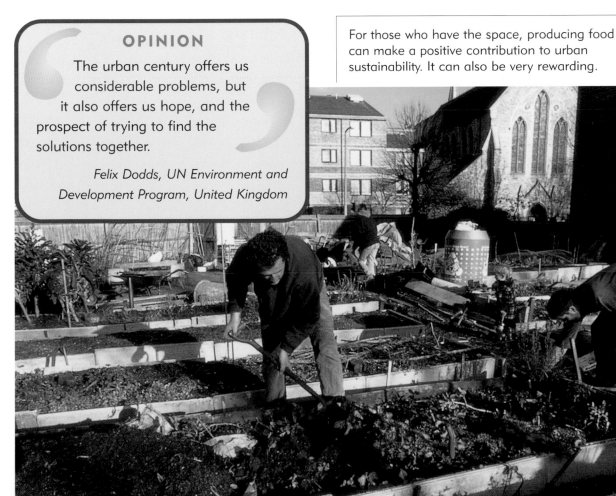

The future of sustainable cities

THE FUTURE IS FULL OF UNKNOWNS for most of us, but one thing that is certain is that the world will become a more urban place to live. Already close to half the world's people live in cities and by the time your children reach your age now, it is likely to be nearer two-thirds.

New housing in Guangzhou, China. As urban space runs short the city is growing upward instead of outward, but how sustainable is such growth?

STILL GROWING

People continue to move toward the world's towns and cities, especially in less-developed countries that are still predominately rural. The speed with which countries are urbanizing is now slowing, but the enormous numbers that have already moved to towns and cities means that most of the world's future population growth will be in the world's urban centers. This will make the provision of safe housing and basic services such as water and sanitation a major challenge for the next few decades. Food, too, will be a challenge and urban agriculture will come to play an increasingly important role in meeting the demand.

This street scene in Shinjuku, Japan, shows how cities can be designed as pleasant and interesting places where people want to live and work.

NEW DIRECTIONS

Some experts believe that continued urbanization is a major problem, but the evidence shows that it need not be. In fact, if carefully managed (as shown by the examples in this book), towns and cities can lead the world toward a more sustainable future. They represent a wealth and variety of ideas gathered together in one location, and with strong leadership and active participation, ideas can quickly be put into practice. Urban centers that have embraced sustainable urbanization show that people benefit as well as the environment. Cities become healthier and wealthier places to live. As incomes and living conditions improve, some problems decrease, such as crime and violence, which are most often caused by the stark inequalities found in urban centers.

Cities can become places in which children and adults enjoy living. They can be a celebration of different cultures and an exhibition of how people can work with, and not against, the environment upon which we all depend. Governments will need to help in turning such a vision into a reality and people of all backgrounds will have to cooperate for the common good of themselves and of their future generations. There is little that can be done to stop urbanization, but people have the power to turn it into a sustainable and rewarding process.

Glossary

Bio-fuels Natural fuels consisting of biological matter (such as wood, crop stalks, animal dung, and collected leaves) or derived from such matter (including ethanol made by fermenting corn and methane gas generated from decomposing biological matter).

Biosphere The part of the earth, atmosphere, and sea that is inhabited by living things.

Car pool A system in which people share the use of cars in order to reduce the number of vehicles on the road, share costs, and limit the environmental impact of motor vehicle emissions.

Cholera Disease of the intestines, often fatal if the person infected does not receive appropriate treatment. It is caused by food or water contaminated with cholera bacteria.

Compost A mixture of organic household waste (e.g. vegetable waste and brown cardboard) and plants that has decomposed over time.

Congestion Where vehicles overcrowd a street or road making movement difficult or impossible for some time. Sometimes called traffic jams.

Developed countries The wealthier countries of the world including Europe, North America, Japan, Australia, and New Zealand.

Eco-cities A term used to describe a growing number of cities that are following the principles of sustainable development.

Ecological footprint The area of land required to provide a population (such as a city) with the resources they consume and to absorb the wastes that they produce.

Ecosystem The contents of an environment, including all the plants and animals that live there. This could be a garden pond, a forest, or the planet Earth.

Emissions Waste products (gases, liquids, or solids) that are released into the environment. For example, motor vehicle exhausts release carbon dioxide, carbon monoxide, and oxides of nitrogen. Some motor vehicles still use gasoline with lead added to it, which means that their emissions include lead.

Fossil fuels Fuels from the fossilized remains of plants and animals formed over millions of years. They include coal, oil, and natural gas.

Greenbelt Land, normally around the edge of an urban area that has special laws to protect it from urban development.

Greenhouse gases Atmospheric gases that trap some of the heat radiating from the Earth's surface.

Immune Protected against a particular disease.

Infant Mortality Rate (IMR) The number of children out of every one thousand live births who die before reaching the age of one.

Infrastructure Networks that enable communication, people, transportation, and the economy to function, such as roads, railways, electricity, phone lines, and water pipelines.

Local Agenda 21 A plan of action that involves local people in finding ways to promote greater care of the local environment and natural resources in the twenty-first century.

Mega-cities Cities that have a population of greater than 10 million inhabitants.

Municipal Relating to the local government of a borough, town, or city or occasionally a region.

Organic A product of living organisms that occurs naturally in the environment.

Parasites Organisms (living things) that live on or in other plants and animals. They can often cause infections or harm to their hosts.

For further exploration

Photovoltaic (PV) cells Cells that convert the sun's energy into an electrical current.

Refugees People who are forced to move from their homes due to circumstances that threaten their well-being (i.e. political conflict or drought)

Renewable resources Resources that can be reused through careful management (e.g. timber and other forest products if forests are replanted as they are used) or that are unaffected by human use (e.g. the energy of the sun or wind).

Resources The materials and energy used in making products or providing services.

Sanitation system The provision of a hygienic toilet and facilities for washing to prevent the spread of diseases associated with human waste.

Self-sufficiency The ability to provide what is needed, e.g. food, resources, energy, etc., without having to rely on external sources.

Sewage Waste carried by sewers. Normally includes human wastes and water, but can include chemicals from homes, offices, and factories.

Slums A word used to describe urban settlements with poor quality and often makeshift and over-crowded housing. Slums normally house the poorest members of society and lack basic services.

Solar power Electricity generated by converting the energy from the sun using solar panels.

Sustainable development Development that can be maintained over time without compromising the ability to meet future needs.

Transit The movement of passengers by local public transportation system.

Urbanization The process by which population gradually becomes more concentrated in towns and cities (urban areas).

Books to Read

Brian Knapp. *World Geography: Cities of the World and Their Future*. Oxfordshire, United Kingdom: Atlantic Europe Publishing Co. Ltd, 1994.

Sally Morgan. *Sustainable Future: Homes and Cities*. London: Franklin Watts, 2002.

Philip Parker. *Project Eco-city: Global Cities*. London: Hodder Wayland, 1994.

Stephanie Turner. *Earth Alert!: Settlements*. London: Hodder Wayland, 2001.

Index